QUEST

FOR THE

"W"

QUEST

FOR THE

"W"

WHEN WINNING IS EVERYTHING

Indy Lindsey

Atlanta, Georgia
Printed in the United States of America

Copyright © 2017 by Indy Lindsey

All rights reserved. Written permission must be secured from the publisher to use or reproduce any part of this book, except for brief quotations in critical reviews and articles.

Published in the United States of America, by ND Playground

Unless otherwise indicated, scripture is taken from the King James, and New King James version of the Bible, from public domain of Bible Gateway.

ISBN: 978-0-9980177-0-9

ISBN: 978-0-9980177-1-6 (ebook)

DEDICATION

I would like to dedicate Quest for the 'W' to my children, because through good and bad, their actions helped to inspire me, and for that I'm grateful. I love you!

A special thanks to my oldest son, Regus. Thank you for being my biggest supporter. You cheered me on through my valley experience when I was stricken with dismay. You always acknowledged my tireless efforts and sleepless nights when working on this book because you saw my vision. It meant the world! Thank you and I love you.
To Vesta, my day 1, thanks for being a loyal best friend. I love you girl.

To the boys, Cam and Chaz, I love you guys and remember that you can do anything you set your mind to doing.

Malik, my ride or die, your love is a constant motivation. I love you!

To all my supporters, I hope this book inspires you, motivates you, make you laugh and most importantly, help place you in position to win.

TABLE OF CONTENTS

Acknowledgements ... 1

Introduction ... 5

Chapter 1 The Image ... 7

Chapter 2 The Job ... 15

Chapter 3 The Hustle ... 23

Chapter 4 The Friendship ... 37

Chapter 5 The Family ... 47

Chapter 6 The Game ... 57

Chapter 7 The Booty ... 65

Chapter 8 The Relationship ... 73

Chapter 9 The Fear & The Faith ... 97

Chapter 10 The Growth (The W) ... 105

End Notes ... 109

About The Author ... 111

ACKNOWLEDGEMENTS

First And Foremost, I thank God for never giving up on me and loving me when I truly didn't deserve it. You have been my rock during my weakest moments in life and I thank you Jesus. You never cease to amaze me! As an adolescent, I had hopes of writing one day, but never followed through. You knew my passion, gave me the vision, and placed me in position for it to finally come to pass. My love for you is infinite.

Secondly, I want to thank my mom, although you are no longer here on this earth, I know you're smiling down on me. You always said, I can do anything I set my mind to doing. Your weaknesses during your struggles when I was growing up helped to make me stronger. You did the best you knew how with what you were given. Words cannot express how much I love and miss you, Mom.

Third, I want to thank my family that I rarely

get to see, because in some form or fashion each of you impacted my life. Gabrielle (my Munchiedo), Raja, Malachi, Isaiah, Amethyst, Anteria, Mia, sisters, brothers, nieces and nephews. Just because you're out of sight, does not mean you're out of mind. I love you.

Next, I want to thank my sister, Mary. Growing up we were two peas in a pod. Wherever I went, most of the time you were sure to follow. We started this journey together with our books. I know I constantly nag you about your procrastination, but that's because I want you to live up to your full potential little sis. Life has been something serious for us, but our best and brightest days are still ahead. I love you!

Finally, I want to thank the man who told me to keep my head up. He taught me that it was ok to ask if I didn't know because even the genius ask questions. Yes, I'm talking about Tupac Shakur. Words cannot express what you mean to me because of the impact you made in my life. Through a very dark period in my life when my father and I could not see eye to eye, your lyrics and interviews helped to transform my life. Your honesty and transparency were beyond refreshing because you shared with the world who you were even though many took it for granted, I embraced it. You taught me that against all odds it was ok to stand up for what I believe. Most importantly, you taught me to stay true to myself. Yes, sometimes my big mouth gets me in trouble, but when I'm right, I refuse to be silenced. Sometimes when I feel like throwing in the towel, all I can hear you saying is handle it, so I do! Thank you, Pac, for being my ambassador of subjectivity. My love for you is immeasurable. Long live 'The Realest'. .

INTRODUCTION

A Quest Is about seeking something of importance to the individual. That quest may be a journey for happiness, success, stability or perhaps a relationship. Some of you may ask, what is a "W" (pronounced dub) A "W" is a win or the willingness to win. In life, we all strive in some form or fashion to be victorious in our endeavors regardless to what they are and ultimately, we are all not that different, just our tactics when it comes to winning. We attempt to place ourselves in situations that we believe will allow us to be successful not fully contemplating the outcome. I'm a firm believer that negative thinking patterns are often the root of the problem and produces failure because our actions are direct results of our thoughts. Let's be honest, when it comes to the end-result, sometimes people set aside morals all in the name of the W that they seek.

The question to ponder is 'what methods

should I use?' Our knowledge and experiences in life provides us with a plethora of options; however, the methods in which we explore those options are left up to us and sometimes we fail to make the best choices. It doesn't matter the obstacles at that given time because all we envision is winning. Throughout the journey of life many challenges arise and often become setbacks. In that moment, we either become defeated or use those trials as motivation to conquer the quest. There comes a time when we must decide if we will be the title of the story or just a mere footnote. Hopefully this book will be somewhat of a jewel and allow you to see things from a unique perspective. We all may come from different walks of life but we all want to win; therefore, it's not too late to be on your quest for the W.

CHAPTER 1

THE IMAGE

In the world of today one's image has become extremely polarizing. The entertainment industry has established a stigma that young women must look a certain way or be a certain type to be impactful. That is by far the biggest misconception of reasoning and unfortunately has left a negative connotation on many women.

To be impactful on a positive level there must first be self-love and sense of direction.

Some women fail to realize that perception of self, is a key factor to the overall image.

SELF-IMAGE

To embrace our image, we must start with self-awareness. It is imperative to know who we are, what we have been through, and how we overcame those challenges. Often, life experiences can impact our lives without us being knowledgeable of what's taking place thus causing low self-esteem and lack of self-worth. Most negative experiences such as, bullying, molestation, abusive relationships, and family issues, can have a direct impact on how we feel about ourselves. Such experiences can leave a negative imprint in our lives, unfortunately, not all encounters are good ones but it is how we channel the energy from those situations that will allow us to embrace who we are and focus on the betterment of self.

Regardless to the situations that have taken place in our lives, we must view ourselves as worthy. Some may ask, 'how can I be worthy when I've been treated as less'? The answer is very simple, develop the confidence needed to propel you to greatness. It must come from within and you must learn to love yourself despite what you have been through. Turn the negative energy into positive energy. Do not allow negative situations to dictate who you are or where you want to be in life. Confidence is essential in being productive individuals because self-image has an impact on our happiness. If we do not believe that we are worthy of acceptance, then how can we expect others to believe?

LOST GIRL

What do you think the self-image of a little girl growing up in a household with an abusive step-father would be? Imagine her innocence slipping away as she watches her mother getting abused and her mother's means of escape becomes alcohol. The step-father decides to up the ante by eventually making advances toward the little girl. She refuses to succumb to his requests so the physical abuse begins. The little girl feels helpless because her mom is in no position to help so she takes her cry for help to a friend. The child is freed from the situation, but the psychological damage had already been done. With no father in her life to teach her the value of love from a man she wonders aimlessly during adolescence on a quest to find it.

PERCEPTION OF OTHERS

Many often concern themselves with how others view them and it causes them to make changes that aren't necessary. A prime example is the size of a woman. Society has placed a stigma on many women that are oversized because it is not deemed to be the ideal image. Another example that has become an epidemic in young women of today to feel good about themselves is getting butt injections or implants. It totally baffles me why women would go through such extremities to gain approval. By no means am I saying that there is anything wrong with enhancing who you are if it makes you feel better about yourself. The point I am conveying is women who are affected by such perceptions resort to different measures of surgical procedures not considering the long-term ramifications when altering the body.

Self-love should not come with a price that could result in botched surgeries or ultimately, death. First, you must love yourself enough to see yourself as beautiful just the way you are. Second, if something becomes a dominating factor in your life that is causing you unhappiness then find a healthy solution to become a happier you. If someone says that your stomach is fat, does that automatically convey that you need to get liposuction or some sort of surgery to reduce the fat? Absolutely not! That is simply an opinion. If you are comfortable with the way your stomach looks, then nothing needs to be done because you are content with the way it looks; however, if your stomach fat has bothered you all along and an outside opinion made you feel compelled to do something then try some healthy exercises that will get you the results you desire. Here's a better example to drive home the point. If someone stated to you that they hated your skin color, does that mean you should bleach your skin or darken it to appease them? Others perception of you should not be a determining factor because their opinion does not make it factual and can often be very distorted.

Our strengths and weaknesses become a direct manifestation of how we view ourselves, how we perform and how others value us. There is always room for improvement, but the improvement needed should be something you deem necessary and not someone else. Perception of yourself will directly impact your self-image therefore, a full assessment of self, will allow you to look at your potential and assets while also examining your limitations and liabilities. Focus on the things that you offer, then the things you desire to work on by setting realistic healthy goals to become a better you. A quick fix by someone's else standards or views can lead to disruptive behavior like alcohol abuse, drug addiction, eating disorders or suicide.

You keep the power by knowing that you are worthy. Sure, we all want to look in the mirror and be happy with what we see, but it must first ignite from within. Imagine everyone walking around looking, acting, dressing and working the same. How boring would that be? We were uniquely and beautifully created therefore, we must embrace those differences. Positive self-image allows us to operate on a higher frequency emotionally, physically, mentally, spiritually and socially. Do not allow others to dictate what you should look like to feel good about yourself. Acceptance of ourselves is the key element to getting the W.

PUBLIC IMAGE

Public image can be a bit tricky because some people put on a facade to display an exterior to capture the attention of others which can often be ingenuine. The fact of the matter is we want to remain true to who we are when it comes to our public image. Don't get me wrong, I'm not saying that when it comes to a job interview or business endeavor that we shouldn't dress for the occasion or conduct ourselves accordingly; quite the contrary, we should be our absolute best.

    Refining our demeanor is often necessary when it comes to social functions, but it's imperative to not lose who we are while doing so, because it helps to develop character. We want to be known for who we are and not what others want us to be. Sure, there is always room for growth and development for each of us, but allow it to be your decision and not the decision of someone who wants to pass judgement on your character. Embrace who you are while figuring out the adjustments that will enhance your growth. Another pandemonium that has consumed today's society is designer labels. People seem to lose their minds when it comes to 'keeping up with the Joneses' and what they're wearing. Is there a problem with adorning ourselves with wonderful things? Absolutely, not! The problem that I've seen with some people is the chasing of those labels and neglecting their responsibilities.

If you can afford the labels you see celebrities, entertainers and rappers wear and talk about then kudos to you, but if your budget does not accommodate such things then you need to prioritize and take care of your responsibilities. If you can afford the attire of the upper echelon without having to sacrifice a necessity then by all means, enjoy it to the fullest.

In any case, when it comes to labels whether you over extend your finances or you have money to blow, do not allow materialistic items to define who you are as a person. Your confidence should be so immense that you can wear the cheapest of items and still look like a star. Your image begins with how you feel about yourself and does not include allowing others to dictate what defines you. In understanding this ideology then you are off to a great start for being a happier you. Understanding who you are will enable you to live on a purpose and be on a quest for the W.

CHAPTER 2

THE JOB

Many Of Us have had to work at some point in our lives. It may have been out of pure necessity, but nevertheless, it had to be done. Not all work experiences will be the same because if you do not love what you do or it's not what you envisioned then more than likely it will not last long.

I've had a couple of experiences that left a sour taste in my mouth as I'm sure some of you can relate. The companies that do not appreciate their employees or the companies with the messy people that want to see you fail are nothing more than a stumbling block. (Urban dictionary calls these type of people Petty Betty's)

Those stumbling blocks can become stepping stones if you pay attention to the lessons you take away from the experience.

During these experiences, I had to work through pettiness, racial tensions, jealousy and pure ignorance. Thankfully, I have the mentality of a warrior; therefore, I would not allow weak attempts to destroy my character to go unanswered. Unfortunately, everyone doesn't have tough skin so it's important to understand your worth in the workforce and the intricate factors that can become a hindrance to your quest.

RESEARCH THE COMPANY

When it comes to working for a company it is extremely important to do your research if you want to put yourself in position to win. I recommend researching the company prior to interviewing. Look for reviews left by consumers or past employees. The reviews will provide insight as to how the company treats their employees and consumers. With the technology of today, it's very easy to retrieve information about a company. I would recommend following the company on social media to interact with current or past employees.

You want to find out how long the company has been in business because there are a ton of companies in existence only for the short-term gain. Other concerns should be the company's policies, culture and environment to see if they align with your expectations and abilities. If there are policies in place that are a direct contradiction to your moral compass, abilities or beliefs then for sure that company is not for you. I do understand that sometimes the economy can place us in tough situations and we find ourselves settling for what comes first. At one point, that was the story of my life. My need for work to support my family took precedence over everything else.

    I've accepted jobs that didn't pay the fair market value to their employees. In doing so, I found myself still struggling to make ends meet. Eventually those conditions led to a hustler's mentality (we'll discuss in a later chapter) because the job failed to deliver. I allowed my financial need to supersede my career goals which became a major hindrance for my growth within a company. If you are not dealing with an economic hardship, yet striving to make a career within a company, by all means, conduct the needed research. Know the company for which you are willing to dedicate your time to ensure it will be a good fit for you and your livelihood. You don't want to find yourself stuck at a job that does not appreciate what you bring to the table because it will directly impact your life in a negative manner. You will find yourself spreading negative vibes and often upsetting those around you because you are unhappy with your job.

THINE COIN (THE PAY)

Needless to say, the pay often becomes a determinant that sometimes allow our tolerance on a job to extend further than the norm. It's easier to stay at a job that you hate when you consider the responsibility that awaits you. It is that type of anticipated thinking that companies thrive on to further their revenue without adjusting for the employee's need. When members of a company feel as if you need them then there's no desire to implement change.

It's important that you keep the power by knowing your worth, doing your research, and knowing what you bring to the table. Not everyone was meant to work for someone else. Some people were designed to be their own boss. In all honesty, you either become an entrepreneur or you work for one. If you are not the entrepreneurial type then always conduct a fair market value analysis on the company to ensure that wages are comparable to what other companies pay in the same field. You must also factor in your education and experience because it significantly increases your value.

Knowing the pay scale for which you qualify plus what you bring to the table places you at an advantage because now you are ready to negotiate your coinage. It is important to not settle for pennies on the dollar because such decisions will impact your quality of life. It is very easy to accept the average, but if your experience is above entry level then your pay should be also. If you have a degree that took tireless hours of challenging work to achieve, then by no means should your pay be the same as a high school graduate. Establish your position by not allowing the company to be the predator and you the mere prey.

THE WORK ENVIRONMENT

When you consider going to a job where you will spend half of your waking hours you must be mindful of the work environment. Unfortunately, at some point in life you may find yourself on a job where the work environment is toxic. It is then you must weigh your options; if you do not wish to keep yourself in a situation where you are experiencing emotional or physical effects from the job.

You will discover that not everyone on the job has your best interest at heart. Sure, there may be some wonderful co-workers on the job that make going to work an easy task, but if the best thing about your job is the end of your shift, then surely there's a problem. Have you ever worked under a narcissistic leader? These types of leaders may come under the title of team lead, supervisor or manager and they possess the ability to create a toxic workplace because they are all about themselves. They often relate to others in a manner that's condescending. Furthermore, they cross boundaries and manipulate others to ensure they come out on top. Such traits with these types of leaders destroy trust and eventually teamwork deteriorates because they cause division among co-workers thus, causing a high turnover rate.

There should always be redeeming qualities on your job that motivate you to be successful; however, if the people, atmosphere or work overshadow those qualities in a negative way and lead to dismay, then it is time to evaluate your choice of employment because the outcome could result in disruptions to your daily life. Have you ever had a complaint about your leader or supervisor and it appeared to have fallen upon deaf ears? Nothing was done to address the complaint about the behavior of that leader in question. It places you in a vulnerable position because upper management does nothing to resolve the matter then you find yourself becoming the primary target of that leader more than ever.

I found myself in an analogous situation and the job that I initially loved became the workplace from hell. I was trying to make the best out of an unpleasant situation so I stayed around because I thought the toxic environment was manageable but eventually came to the realization that it was no longer tolerable for me. I saw people stay with the company despite the toxic environment. Some were intimidated by the connections of the supervisor within the company, whereas others felt they needed the job and didn't realize their worth. I worked on another option, my plan b, that would allow me to make my exit so I submitted my letter of resignation. Can you believe upon submitting my resignation the narcissism of the leaders came to the forefront? Instead of accepting my two weeks' notice they decided to terminate me under a false premise. Their ignorance brings me to my next point.

Documentation of everything is necessary when you work in a toxic environment. I can't emphasize enough the importance of a paper trail. In my situation, policies were always changing so it became necessary to document everything to stay well-informed. Keep a record of one on one meetings and policy changes because it offers a level of defense. Managers can argue that their policy says one thing when it in fact doesn't. Because of my documentation, I was victorious over the narcissistic leaders that came for me with the foolery.

Working under someone else is not meant for everyone, therefore, options must be explored. We must learn to remove limits from our lives and think outside of the box. Discover what your niche is and develop the necessary skills to place yourself in a position of winning. Entrepreneurship is growing daily and can be an overwhelming feat, but the freedom that it brings is well worth it in the end. Due to today's technology, options are limitless. In business, you will have two choices; you can either become an entrepreneur and be your own boss or work for someone that became an entrepreneur. Wherever your journey may lead you ensure there is a vision because with no vision the people perish. (Prov. 29:18)

CHAPTER 3

THE HUSTLE

As Previously Stated not everyone was designed to work for someone else and may not be ready to run an organized business. So, what other options are available? I strongly believe that everyone has a talent of some sort and should utilize those skills to the fullest potential. Figure out what drives you, and use it as a means to create a consistent cash flow and in doing so you will have created a hustle. It's important to allow your creativity to fuel your hustle.

To hustle effectively you must have self-determination, courage and confidence to generate the momentum needed to make certain your hustle becomes profitable. Different people try different things some legal some illegal. Let's be honest, in many instances, illegal hustles do not lead to a successful outcome. It's important to know the direction your hustle will lead you so, think like a boss, especially if you're on a quest for a W.

SELLING DRUGS

People take different measures to obtain money for varied reasons. I am not here to pass judgement on anyone for the methods they use to support their families. My goal is help them explore other means that will ensure their freedom and livelihood.

    Selling Drugs has been an adaptable hustle for many decades and doesn't appear to be going away anytime soon. I wonder why? The sad thing about the drug hustle is it captures the attention of the misguided youth and they use it as a means of income. That should never be the case for anyone because it seldom ends well. The drug hustle leads to a life of fast money, but with that money comes the concerns of prison life. Furthermore, when you are hustling drugs and living the life, there's always someone sitting back, watching your moves, and planning their attack to take what you've grinded for. Yes, sadly enough, it's happened far too many times because everyone wants to be a kingpin totally disregarding the value of another's life. In the words of battle rapper,

Loaded Lux, "Is your money being long, worth your life span being shorter?" Ponder That!

Entertainers, primarily rappers, tirelessly tell stories about selling drugs but what they fail to do is enlighten you about the disadvantages that comes with the territory. In my opinion, to engage in selling drugs is a selfish act. Let me explain... Not only do you put your freedom at risk but you put the lives of others that matter to you in harm's way.

It takes strong willed individuals to rise above the enticements that have been strategically placed for you to embrace. Just because you see it taking over your surroundings does NOT mean you should become a product of your environment. Ask yourself, 'To enforce change does my community need another frail follower or a solid leader?' We will always face adversity, but how we overcome it is what matters. The infamous Tupac Shakur once said, "I know it seems hard sometimes but remember one thing, through every dark night, there's a bright day after that. So, no matter how hard it get, stick your chest out, keep ya head up and handle it."

LOST GIRL (NO HOPE IN DOPE)

Remember the little girl who spent her adolescence wondering aimlessly? She eventually located her father and attempted to build a relationship with him. In her mid-twenties, she relocated to the city where he lived trying to continually build the relationship. Things didn't go as she envisioned and it stirred up rebellion within her. She became engulfed with bitterness, disappointment and depression due to her father's inability to love her as she deserved. She redirected her attention to the dope dealers. For some odd reason, she always had a fascination with drug dealers, perhaps it was the never-ending hustle that gained her attention. While dating the dope boys she was very attentive. She observed the process, learned the movements and established the connects. She was preparing for her journey in the dope game. One day through a mutual friend, she met the woman that became her 'drug selling mentor' and her hustle elevated to a new level. She taught her how to setup shop in the drug house in case the police raided.

    Although they sometimes bumped heads, they formed an amazing friendship and took the game by storm. One evening her friend borrowed her car for a drug pickup and never returned. She was furious because she didn't know where her car was and the mentor she now called friend was not returning calls. It wasn't until the next morning that she discovered her friend was killed while sitting in the car. The guy with her returned unharmed and gave his rendition of sequence of events, but it fell upon deaf ears. How could she be shot dead while sitting in the car but he was still breathing? His story did not add up. Devastated by what had taken place she became withdrawn from everyone. As time passed, mutual friends approached her suggesting she operate the 'hustle house' because the clientele had already established a rapport with her and trusted her. She accepted the offer not realizing that there was more to lose than to gain.

 She loved the money and perks that came with hustling dope. One night while sitting upstairs counting her money, she heard loud thumps and the sound of voices through the monitor yelling 'get down, get down'. She realized that it was the task force and everything her mentor taught her went into action. She tossed the remainder of dope she had left out of a window that she left slightly lifted, hid her money and gun and pretended to watch television. By some miracle, she was not arrested. After about 2 weeks of letting things cool down at the 'hustle house' it was back to business as usual. The fast money enticed her so she was not easily deterred.

 One day she was stopped by a friend on her way to grind and was warned that some guys planned to rob her later that night. She did not allow it to stop her hustle because wherever she went, her gun went also. Later that night she received a call warning her not to leave to go home because several guys were outside the house in bushes waiting to rob her. She became nervous so she called her boyfriend and explained what was communicated to her. She asked him to ride through the neighborhood and check out the scenery. He drove pass the house and confirmed that several guys were outside lurking. He advised her to lock up shop, stay upstairs, and keep the gun cocked.

    Can you imagine the thoughts in her head? She was petrified but refused to be paralyzed by fear. She announced to her runner that no one was to come upstairs or she would shoot through the door. Shop was closed! The next morning, after what seemed to be the longest night of her life, she had her runner and others to verify that the coast was clear. Once they checked the surroundings and gave her the clearance she left the 'hustle house' and that ended her plight in selling drugs. After losing a friend to the hustle, task force kicking in doors and envious dudes planning her demise, she realized that being around to raise her son and daughter was more important than fast money.

PONZI SCHEMES AND INVESTMENT SCAMMERS

These types of hustles tremendously affect people daily and the victims never see it coming until it is too late. Imagine someone soliciting you for a generous sum of money about a business venture and promising a high return on the investment within a brief period. It gives the impression its fair enough if he or she can provide documentation to support the financial claims, right?

Here's the clincher, the hustler never invests the money that you've provided; however, does pay out dividends to you. It appears that you're on a fast track to making a ton of money. Totally the opposite! The hustler generally pays out dividends to the investor that was collected from new investors. The gesture of good faith tactic. At this point, word of mouth from the happy investor is underway and new investors are encouraged to invest. The cycle continues until the hustler is no longer able to obtain funding from new investors to pay out dividends to old investors. Another option is the hustler takes all the money and move on to the next victim. How terrible is that?

I can't speak for anyone else, but I work hard for my money and I tread very cautiously when it comes to making investments. If you are skeptical when it comes to an investment, do the research before handing over any money. There are tools available that will provide insight prior to investing. Conduct thorough research on the individual attempting to solicit funds from you. Ask question and take notes. Find out if the investment is registered and get a full understanding of that investment. If there are red flags then by no means should you move forward with investing.

This type of hustle is not only illegal, but a depravation of morals and values. I deem it worse than selling drugs because the victim is being deceived thus, not allowing him or her to make a rational decision about the investment as opposed to a drug dealer that's operating off a supply and demand type hustle. Anyone can become vulnerable and fall victim to the investment hustle but, the primary targets for such scams are retirees and elderly people. There is no honor in such thievery because the victim is being deceived and taken advantage of without full disclosure.

If that has been a hustle that you've used to your advantage then it's time to reevaluate your hustling options. If you possess the skills to swindle copious amounts of money from the gullible, imagine the heights you could soar by allowing those skills to legally and morally place you in a position of winning.

ESCORTS, PROSTITUTES AND STRIPPERS

Many will argue that escorts, prostitutes and strippers are all in different leagues. There may be many differences but the similarities are uncanny. Prostitute is the term given to females of a lower-class, who generally exchange sexual favors for minimal cash, whereas, escort is the name associated with those whom consider themselves to be of a higher caliber. They often exchange various favors for large sums of money. As for strippers, well, they have no preference because they take it off for everyone and the right price can lead to a secluded room for one on one pleasure. Let's cut to the chase, on various occasions many of them sell the goods just for different prices.

Escorting is not deemed illegal because it caters to the upper echelon and classifies services rendered as companionship. Neither is stripping considered illegal because they are stripping down to their bare skin and showcasing their 'bodily talents. I've decided to group them together because the commonality is moral deprivation and the chase for the dollar. Morality is but a deterrent when individuals want immediate gratification to appease their livelihoods.

We may never fully understand the determining factors that cause women to feel inclined to use their bodies as objects to gain materialistic contentment, but we must make a concerted effort to consider the possible need they're attempting to fulfill. I struggle with accepting the idea that it's done just for the hell of it. Perhaps they are not aware of the talents they possess and not everyone knows how to properly hustle so they turn to the assets they consider valuable to generate a form of revenue. Whatever the reason, an alternative means of hustling must be adapted that doesn't depreciate the value of the woman. When you understand your self-worth then anything that depreciates your value becomes an impediment.

We must not be so quick to condemn either. Let me explain. Many strippers, escorts, and even prostitutes have been able to build a brand for themselves using social media and reality television as an outlet to become productive individuals. Let's salute them for wanting better for themselves and realizing that even though it's glorified in the entertainment industry of today as a 'rite of passage' they do not have to be less and remain demoralized in order to become more and reach great heights. Winning is not easy, but you have an option to create the blueprint that will propel you to greatness.

ONLINE HUSTLES

There are massive amounts of online hustles available to those looking to make some money legally. The possibilities are endless! If you are looking to start an online retail business and desire your own website, no worries! There are several websites that will allow you to create a free website for your business. A free website helps to minimize your startup costs by freeing up money for you to purchase wholesale merchandise. That's just one way to hustle online. Let's discuss online hustling from a broader spectrum. Perhaps you don't want a website, but have a plethora of items you would like to sell. There are a ton of websites that cater to such desires. Some may charge a small fee upon completion of sale like eBay, Amazon, and Etsy just to name a few, but you choose your selling method, list your items and wait for the sells to come in. How difficult is that?

Another online hustle is blogging. It has taken the internet by storm because everyone has a story to tell. Why not get paid for something you love doing? If you love writing or doing videos, then this is a legit hustle made for you. Make money from the comfort of your own home or on the go. I'm not a blogger, but the logistics of blogging does require dedication as does any successful venture. Start by freelance blogging, then promote it via social media to build your audience. Once you establish a client base, then you can decide the number of blogs you wish to write monthly for paying clients. If you decide to make it a full-time hustle, the profits have the potential to be very satisfying. Then, of course, there's video blogging or vlogging. Once you build your audience, the clicks will bring the pay. I know several people that have made blogging their full-time jobs and live a very comfortable life. Hustling is a lifestyle and doesn't have to resort in compromising your integrity.

OTHER AVENUES OF HUSTLING

If you have the survivor instinct within, then you know how to generate revenue through hustling. It's an innate ability to ensure that you are able to support yourself and family. Some people choose the wrong means for hustling, but nevertheless, they do what they deem necessary at that given time. Let's look at some other avenues of legitimate hustling. If you are tech savvy, then computer repairs may be a profitable hustle for you. Just about everyone uses computers and when the computer gets a virus or crashes they need someone to get it up and running again. That's where you come in. Getting paid for something you love doing. Can you say winning?

Of course, there are the mechanics. We need them to keep our cars running smoothly. Speaking of cars, there are services available that will pay you to drive people to their destinations. That is, if you like driving and can tolerate traffic. We certainly can't forget the handyman that possess the skills to repair just about anything in the home. He/she is known as the 'jack of all trades' and is not limited to just one task. Hustling has been around since forever and isn't going anywhere anytime soon. Your hustle should be conducive to your lifestyle, but if it jeopardizes your freedom or integrity, you may want to rethink your decision. Ultimately, we are all accountable for our own actions, just ensure that the outcome from your choice of hustling doesn't do more harm than good.

CHAPTER 4

THE FRIENDSHIP

I Believe It's fair to say that most people have individuals in their lives whom they consider friends, right? If you reflect on your childhood and forward to your present state of being you can compartmentalize those individuals. Some may have stood the test of time whereas others may have fallen by the way side. Either way, those considered friends should complement who you are today and bring out the very best in you. Naturally, you will not always agree on everything, but despite differences, you know beyond a shadow of a doubt they love you unconditionally.

That type of friend is hard to come by and should not only be appreciated but kept close to heart. I've had a significant amount of people in my life that I once considered friends, but for distinct reasons, not all stood the test of time. As time progresses throughout life we often learn the brutal truth… not everyone is genuine or has our best interest at heart. Because a successful quest requires us to focus on our goals with a positive mindset, we must surround ourselves with people who desire to see us succeed.

THE ACQUAINTANCE (ASSOCIATES)

These types of friends are people that may be in your presence from time to time and possibly fun to be around when you see them, but, they do not know you on an intimate level. Perhaps you see them on the job or at various events. They superficially converse with you but they're not around enough to establish a solid bond. Acquaintances mainly support your endeavors when there are similar interests. This is mainly noticeable at social functions, business meetings, or gatherings. They generally network by discussing like interests because it allows them to share their views and information on things that can be beneficial to their quest. With this type of friend, limitations are in place because you rarely discuss your personal business with them or call them when you are facing a problem; however, depending on the amount of time spent some acquaintances have the potential of becoming dear friends. It is important to socialize and meet new people because you never know who could end up being that 'ram in the bush' when you need a voice of reasoning.

CONDITIONAL FRIEND

Conditional friends require certain needs being met. You may have established what you believed was a great friendship, until the conditions began to take a toll. They may have been in your life for years and you learned to tolerate the stipulations that were placed, but let's be honest, by no means is it healthy. Conditional friends strongly believe you are supposed to adhere to their way of thinking even if it defies all logic. They do not value strong willed individuals that are capable of thinking for themselves because they prefer 'yes' friends. 'Yes' friends are people that agree with anything they say, and continuously allow conditions to be applied. Have you ever had a conditional friend? If you haven't then you should be thankful because you escaped a never ending tumultuous battle.

I had a conditional friend and as time went by her conditions grew increasingly intolerable. For the longest time, I valued her as a devoted friend because she had been around over a decade. At one point, we did everything together such as;

family outings, vacations, concerts, bar-b-ques, sporting events, and the list goes on. One day she crossed the line by giving me an ultimatum that was beyond ridiculous. That is when I drew the line in the sand. I attempted to reason with her hoping she would see how her demands were distorted and condescending to say the least, but I was unsuccessful in my efforts. I once loved her like a sister, perhaps more, but she was only focused on me seeing her point of view in everything and when I begged to differ, she grew to be more and more disrespectful.

Her conditional friendship forced me to reflect on things that had taken place over several years. In doing so, I came to the realization that our friendship was unhealthy and one-sided because she had been engulfed in emotions filled with negative energy and insecurities. She didn't want a friend that would always be authentic with her, instead she wanted someone that would agree to her terms at all costs because that is what she became accustomed to with her 'yes' friends. That's not who I am nor was I willing to convert by becoming her puppet. Well, needless to say, that friendship was severed because her actions were those of a 'frenemy'.

If you have conditional friends it's time to reevaluate their value and have a heart to heart conversation. If they become more of the problem as opposed to the solution then it's time to part ways. Your quest should include people that want to see you prosper on all levels. Anything that becomes a hindrance on your journey must be alleviated because it's dead weight. Imagine walking on a path that leads to heights you've only dreamed of accomplishing. The extra baggage will become cumbersome and deter you from reaching your destination. You can continue your quest with the extra weight, but you should be prepared for frequent delays.

COUNTERFEIT FRIEND (FRENEMY)

These types of friends are by far the worst because they give the impression that they are genuine when in fact, they can't be trusted. You may have established a long-term friendship with them and shared many secrets, but along the way something went terribly wrong. In many instances, there are psychological issues causing resentment that are rooted from their own regrets, pain, and past experiences. As a result of the lingering issues, their frustrations are directed towards you. The smallest trigger from you can cause an inadvertent reaction because your mere existence causes them tremendous anguish. Perhaps there is hidden jealousy and their train of thought depicts you as a threat.

Clearly, this is the unhealthiest type of friendship and can cause irreversible damage. Frenemies know how to hurt you because you've allowed them to enter your circumference and they know your weaknesses. When opportunity presents itself, they will bring you down. In my experience, I've discovered it's best to steer clear from such people in order to excel and reach your full potential. Do not attempt to be a she-ro or hero by trying to change these individuals. They must take the initiative by acknowledging the problem otherwise, you will find yourself depleted of energy trying to help people that do not want to be helped.

TRUE FRIEND (YOUR DAY ONE)

It goes without saying that a true friend is just that-true! They love you despite your short comings. They embrace who you are and will go the extra mile to see you smile. They are your biggest fan as well as your best critic. They don't have a problem telling you when you messed up yet they love you anyhow. They differ from the other types listed because they support you when there is nothing to gain for them. You can tell them your deepest secret and it's always kept. They are by no means a 'yes' friend because they provide their honest opinion and expect the same in return. Their loyalty is immeasurable and their love knows no boundaries. True friends provide moral, emotional and spiritual support. It may take some people time to grow on you to reach that status whereas others took that position from day one.

Not everyone will be able to relate to the context of this chapter. Perhaps some of you just lump your friends together, but let me reassure you there's a hell of a difference. Take a second to think about it...

Who's that friend that you can call at 3:00 a.m. to come and get you should you be stranded? Who's that friend that will take care of your kids like his or her own? See where I'm going with that?

You may not see that true friend often, but when you do, it's as if no time had elapsed. This is the type of friend you want to cherish because you know beyond a shadow of a doubt they would ride or die with you in any given situation.

I have a variety of friends, but the ones that were not trying to encourage and uplift had to be cut off. Besides, I need zero drama in my life when creating the blueprint that's designed for me to win and neither do you! At some point the weak must become obsolete especially when you are trying to elevate to another level. As for the friends that weathered the storm, they've earned the right to be in your circle as you ascend to new heights.

I have several friends that I consider devoted friends, but one stands out at this very moment.

She and I met under peculiar circumstances and during that time, I had no idea that 20 years later she would be my day one. We've moved to different states and always managed to keep in touch. When I am stressing about anything major she is the one that reminds me that it too shall pass. She is the yin to my yang because we complement one another and are two forces that interact to form a dynamic friendship. I would not trade her for anything in the world.

We have shared one another's pain and because we've faced similar struggles, it's as if our steps became one. We watched each other's growth over the years and often reflect on how far we've come. We are kindred spirits and can sometimes feel when the other needs to hear that uplifting voice or see that comforting face. With her, there are never ultimatums, doubt, backstabbing or threats because it's genuine. We accept one another for who we are and offer encouraging words that will enhance both our growth. This is the type of friend that you need to have in your corner; the type that's your biggest fan, your loudest cheerleader, your confidant, your bridge and your drill sergeant if need be. This kind of friend is not waiting for you at the finish line instead, he or she is running the race with you, cheering you along the way.

CHAPTER 5

THE FAMILY

Family Covers A lot of territory and by far the greatest challenge of them all. We are tied to our families for the rest of our lives and that may or may not be a good thing. We are going to discuss various aspects of family life that affect our quest. I'm the first one to say that family life is not always easy because even though they're family, it doesn't mean they want to see you win.

LOVE, SUPPORT, AND COMMUNICATION

Each of us deserve love and support from our families. It doesn't necessarily mean we are going to get it. Perpetuating factors often become dominant forces that plague many families. The upbringing of individuals impacts the family dynamic. Unfortunately, not everyone comes from a two-parent household which sometimes open the door for struggle; however, contrary to popular belief, not every household requires two parents to create a stable environment full of love, support, and communication. In some cases, long-term friends take on the role of family, perhaps you are closer to them than you are actual family members. Whatever the case may be, it's necessary to differentiate love and support from jealousy and envy.

    Families consist of various members and each are different in their own way. We must first learn to embrace the differences that family members possess because it creates a unique dynamic. We may not always agree with their actions but we need to consider their uniqueness. In doing so, it places us in position to receive and give love accordingly. If we agreed with every decision an individual made within our family then there wouldn't be any adversity to overcome. Families must face challenges to become a stronger unit. If the foundation is built on unadulterated love then everything else will run its course.

    Think about your relationship with different family members. Is each relationship the same? Probably not. You may be closer to a sibling then you are a parent. As odd as it may seem, perhaps that sibling understands your behavior better than your parent would. Does it mean you love your parent less? Does it mean your parent love you less? By no stretch of the imagination does it mean there is less love from either side. Parents often tend to be more structural and enforce rules within the family whereas a sibling may be liberal. Regardless, to the closer connection with any family member there must always be an open line of communication within the family. Effectively communicating leaves no room for the element of surprise and builds a stronger support system. Sure, the outcome may sometimes result in a disagreement, but at least you would have stated your position on the matter and afforded others the opportunity to discuss their concerns.

It is not always easy to co-exist within a family, but we must learn to make decisions that signify cohesiveness especially, if it directly impacts the lives of others within the family. Would you want to be blindsided by someone's actions that resulted in a negative outcome? Absolute not! Instead, you would want to be well informed should such actions result in an undesirable manner, consequently, you are prepared to handle the situation.

When there is a solid foundation on which a family is built, love will surpass every obstacle that falls in the path of that family. Regardless to how rocky the road may get, they have one another to lean on during challenging times and those who are in opposition do not stand a chance. Don't dismiss family members that have been in your corner because of a difference of opinion or struggles. Ultimately, they want to see you win.

FAMILY LOYALTY OR LACK THEREOF

Loyalty is an essential ingredient within a family. With no loyalty, previous bonds that were formed often become damaged. It's important to understand the essence of your family so the expectancies are not misconstrued. Loyal family members display their faithfulness by honoring their obligations and remaining authentic to family traditions. Some may argue that traditions change and in some instances, that would be valid; however, many families thrive on traditions that have been ongoing throughout generations; therefore, it's frowned upon when those traditions are not honored.

Emotional presence during times of duress and triumph is obligatory because it signifies loyalty. Disagreements that may have taken place should be relinquished and unwavering encouragement and support need to be the primary focus during times of need. It is then we must learn to ignore imperfections of family members. Many of us hold our families in high regard that is, until something goes wrong, perhaps a form of betrayal, but we must realize that we are all human and prone to make mistakes.

    People frequently make the error of viewing the functionalities of other family systems by comparing it to theirs. That should never be the case because experiences differ with each individual within a household. Every family has a background, some in which have the best kept little secrets, nevertheless, there is no disgrace in acknowledging that family members have scarred you or you them. What's important is healing, forgiving and striving to rebuild the family dynamic. Without finding a resolution for those transgressions the family loyalty will face imminent danger. Furthermore, not working through the issues and sweeping things under the rug will take on a form of repression which can negatively impact current and future relationships.

    Loyalty within a family is amazing, but it should not be to your detriment. Let me elaborate. If certain family members are a continuous nuisance without acknowledgement and willingness to repair the damages they've caused then by no means should you be the doormat for them to wipe their feet. In my opinion, your sanity supersedes your loyalty to them. They must be willing to do the inevitable...change their erroneous behavior. Hopefully you will examine things in totality and not make the mistake of nurturing people that refuse to implement change. Your loyalty wouldn't be in question; however, their actions would be. Some people simply will not be loyal to anyone, unless, there is a need to be filled. Once that need is met, the loyalty will dissipate.

I've made the mistake of coddling some of my siblings due to my loyalty and in my time of need it wasn't reciprocated. Sure, it disappointed me, but it became a pattern that I allowed to continue from childhood. It wasn't until recent that I came to the realization that it was a case of misplaced loyalty. Change needed to come forth. If I continued to rationalize that enabling them equated to loyalty then they would never take the necessary steps to grow and become productive individuals. In life, we must learn the importance of family regardless to how dysfunctional it may appear.

Some members we must love from afar because their negative energy has the tendency to consume us. It doesn't mean we should love them less; it simply means they need to work on reforming their thought pattern and behaviors. Their only concerns are themselves and loyalty is but a figment of their imaginations. Do you have a family member or two of this kind? Well, I do! The only time they pretend to be loyal is when money is involved. Go figure! You find yourself attempting to reason with that member in hopes of establishing a solid foundation. Your efforts may have worked for a brief period and you were elated that you were on a new-found path.

Those moments were short lived because they reverted to their old habits. If such behavior is tolerated it will become a never-ending cycle. I separated myself from those members because I decided that I wanted more out of life than misery. Misplaced loyalty should never have the power to dictate our paths. Family and loyalty should go hand in hand, unfortunately, that's not always the case. Focus on your vision and those that are supposed to be there will be. Let no one deter you from your quest...not even family.

BETRAYAL

Betrayal has the enormous potential of destroying families. Never does anyone envision people with whom they've entrusted their love betraying or turning their backs on them for outside forces, but it happens. The effects of betrayal leave an emotional impact on the individual betrayed. Disbelief and distress are ever-present. Anger becomes all-consuming and trust is no longer existent. When someone devalues another by betrayal the relationship is severely damaged and in many instances unable to be repaired.

Scenario I
Imagine a family member allowing an outside force to coerce him or her to create a fabricated story that resulted in your arrest. Your relationship was solid with that family member but out of nowhere he or she brings chaos to your life because of a lie due to a difference of opinion. How would you react to that? Let's imagine that you eventually allow that relative to be in your presence again; however, he or she fails to apologize or show remorse for the betrayal. You decide to forgive, but you struggle with the hurt because the individual isn't making a concerted effort to repair the damage; instead, he or she is taking every opportunity to make matters worse by continuously lying, being disrespectful and causing disruption. How can you properly heal from the damage when the family member is not putting forth an effort? You can't, unless the person who initialized the betrayal becomes remorseful and makes a sincere effort to rebuild the relationship. It is then the healing process can begin.

Scenario II
A family member meets someone and immediately jumps into a relationship then move in with the

individual. Neither took the time to get to know one another and it's apparent they have different morals and values. The family member starts to change for the worse to impress the outsider who's morally deprived, conniving and manipulative. The outsider uses seduction and manipulation as a means of control. The family member is captivated by the experience and turns his back on the family along with his children for no apparent reason. All that matters to him is his new-found love and the baggage she came with. The family is taken aback because the unexpected betrayal is unwarranted. Various family members attempt to reach out to him but to no avail. The neglect received from him affected his family tremendously especially his children. He eventually comes to the realization that he misses his family and ask their forgiveness. Can you forgive this type of betrayal that disrupted the family? Absolutely! Because the apology was sincere and followed by effort to rebuild the connection with his family. All can be forgiven and trust can be earned.

Scenario III
An adult family member has been entrusted to care for a younger family member and decides to violate the member by committing egregious acts on the individual. The younger member begins to act out and no one understands why until one

day he/she decides to tell a parent about the acts that have taken place. The parent is outraged and demands answers to understand the pedophilia behavior of the adult family member. The adult family member denies the allegations but the individual to which it occurred is adamant about the veracity of the claim. How does the family overcome this type of betrayal? Such betrayal is prevalent with many individuals and lives are damaged because of it. Even though the individual may suppress the emotions that generated from the betrayal, eventually it will have a direct impact on the decisions he or she makes. Accountability from the offending family member is necessary then perhaps healing can begin. Often, generational curses are passed down to offspring's because issues of betrayal were not acknowledged or addressed accordingly in the past.

CHAPTER 6

THE GAME

When It Comes to gaming everyone wants to win! The challenges are endless, but the victories are sweeter. Egos are stroked when battles are won. We see it throughout various sports when players and fans alike bask in the moment of achievements. With the everchanging technology people can take gaming to new levels. The desire to win is ever present whether it's playing video games, participating in sporting events, or simply gaming to get the girl or guy. What lengths are people willing to go to get the W?

ONLINE GAMING (VIDEO GAMES)

Playing video games have become a favorite

pastime for many people. The feeling of beating the computer in one of your favorite games is indescribable. What happens when you get stuck on a level that you can't seem to bypass? The frustration sets in and you become consumed with winning by any means. The determination intensifies. Now, how many of you have searched for cheat codes to move beyond that level? It happens all the time.

Matter of fact, with the development of online gaming, the battle for victory has never been more aggressive and gamers go to extremes to get the W. There is one cheat code that is always trending when playing 2K (a popular basketball game). I'm sure you gamers know what I'm talking about.... Getting that VC (virtual currency) is a MUST. Instead of going through the process to develop and become better, people take the quick route that requires no effort to obtain immediate gratification. Some may argue that it is not cheating, but if you are paying for an advantage (which some people do) instead of going through the process, then what else would you call it?

Let's say you still disagree that buying VC is cheating. Ok fine. Let's view it like this... Is it deemed okay when athletes take steroids for an advantage? Aha! Absolutely Not! In many instances, they are suspended or fined if not both. In this case, gamers and athletes alike just want to get the W.

THE GAME OF SPORTS

I'm an avid lover of sports especially football and basketball. I'll be the first to admit that the officiating is not always up to par and it directly impacts the game. As a mother of boys that grew up playing sports, there were times when the gym echoed my yells at the referees for the bad calls made. After games, I would ask referees how did they miss certain calls and I distinctly remember them saying 'they call in favor of the more aggressive team'. Now that's food for thought! It wasn't because fouls were not committed, but because the other team played more aggressively. That changed my outlook on sports and taught me to teach my boys to play more aggressive.

I've heard the argument that politics factor into sports and by golly I believe it. I watch sports on both collegiate and national levels and some of the calls or lack of calls are atrocious to say the least, but let's think about the game from the player's perspective. When they go out to play, they are playing for the win and by any means they aim to get it. I remember watching a national football game on Monday night and one of my favorite cornerback players jumped offside and slammed into the knee of the kicker.

Oh, my goodness, that changed the momentum of the game! People were outraged and accused him of cheating as well as the refs. Many argued that it was unnecessary roughness, but from his standpoint he believed the ball was tipped on the play and it was his job to go for the block. He did just that! He's very competitive and believes in doing his job effectively when it comes to getting the W.

There was an incident during a national basketball playoff game where a player was attempting to inbound the ball and avoid the five second violation. He struggled because he received tremendous pressure from the defender; therefore, he leaned over and threw the defender an elbow to create space to get the ball inbounds. The referee was in clear view but failed to make the call.
The team went on to win the game, but had that thrown elbow been called as a foul, arguably, the results may have been different. Perhaps it was the adrenaline rush that impelled the elbow to the defender or just maybe it was his willingness to win the game since it was in very close proximity, either way, he was on a quest and was not going to allow anything or anyone deter his team from getting the W. By no means do I agree with such antics, but I do comprehend the sense of urgency to win.

SPITTING GAME (POWER OF SUGGESTION)

Men and women alike have the tendency to 'spit game' or attempt to use the power of suggestion when someone catches their attention. Let's be clear, not everyone that attempts it will be successful, especially if their approach has no depth. Before approaching the individual that has stimulated your senses, give thought to how you will initiate a conversation and contemplate your response expectancy. Your thought pattern, and behaviors should be conducive to making the expectancy occur. Body language and tone of the recipient requires attentiveness and will help you to identify the suggestions given to you. You must be prepared to counteract suggestions of negativity that you may receive.

Women appreciate men who can anticipate the response they will receive from them because their attitudes, gestures, and tones will be indicative of their consciousness. Allow your confidence to lead the way. Fellas, please stop with the hey baby or the damn you look good! Don't get me wrong, that may work for certain women that are not aware of their worth, but for the women that are conscious of their being and of a different caliber, your efforts will be shot down. Stop being typical! Stand out from other men by showing her the context is more than attempting to get her in bed.

Your conversation should express that you are interested in getting to know who she is and what her interests are. Be creative by adding a little flavor to your conversation and by using descriptive words to drive your point home and arouse her imagination. Women are emotional creatures and process information different than men; therefore, they tend to detect foolishness rather quickly. It's necessary to keep her engaged in conversation that focuses on her attributes and aspirations. In doing so, you just may find a winner.

Women, please stop falling for the demeaning approaches that men spring on you We must train our minds to reject anything that is less than we deserve. It's a dog eat dog world out here; therefore, we must act like a lady but always think like a man. Know what your intentions are prior to approaching him. Men are far more susceptible to game than women because it's in their nature. They have a never-ending vulnerability when it comes to what pleases the eye; therefore, the task is far less challenging. They can be very egotistical so start with a compliment that's sure to make him smile. Once you have his attention, engage him in conversation and remember to stroke his ego throughout. Keep in mind that not all men are alike; therefore, some may require additional work. Preparation is necessary so compile your thoughts, know your strengths, and utilize them by making the power of suggestion work in your favor.

CHAPTER 7

THE BOOTY

Men And Women alike take different avenues when it comes to getting the goods. Some are by happenstance whereas others are due to opportunists seizing the moment. The quest for the flesh fulfillment is all about getting the sex. You may encounter someone and immediately conceive the thought of engaging in intercourse with that person. It's because their physical form aroused your curiosity. Often the need for casual sex becomes sufficient because there's no desire of having a relationship. Of course, that journey can be very satisfying, but everything that glitters isn't gold. There are primarily two common methods for achieving this W and they are face to face and online. Each requires a different approach or technique, but with a little precision, the finesse can lead to a memorable experience.

FACE TO FACE FINESSING

The face to face encounter is the oldie but goodie because it gives you the advantage of seeing your intended target up close and personal. Pictures and filters can't hide what your eyes can clearly see. This approach isn't for the meek and it requires a bit of that je ne sais quoi. The power of suggestion should be in full effect mode to accomplish this feat. The face to face encounter can happen at any given place like a grocery store, sports bar, club, social function or even church. Since this quest is for short term gratification, you're 'A' game is necessary because you never get a second chance to make a first impression. You may run into some roadblocks due to lack of interest from the other party. Should that occur, move on to the next candidate of your choosing. Once you meet someone that reciprocates your interest, move forward with orchestrating a time and location the two of you can get better acquainted. The task at hand is not about spending a life time but rather having a good time.

    Build a rapport and establish a comfort level so the other party feels he or she can freely open up to you and let his or her guard down. Once the guard is lowered, vulnerability opens the door for you to attempt to get the goods. Here's the thing, getting the goods can potentially open Pandora's box. Getting the 'booty' can cause an overflow of emotions, forms of attachment, and sense of entitlement. Well, I bet you were not expecting that, were you? It is always best to set the expectations prior to getting the goods. In doing so, both parties are in agreeance and have a clear understanding about any future dealings or lack thereof. You don't want the individual to stalk your social media or show up at your home unannounced. That could get very messy and result in physical altercations or perhaps worse.

Perhaps your lifestyle keeps you far too busy for a relationship, but sometimes you desire the pleasures of a man or woman without the commitment. Well, that places you in a category of wanting the jewels that he or she has to offer. Many people at some point have taken that path because of the sense of freedom that comes along with it and it allows you to keep your options open. There is nothing wrong with enjoying the pleasures of someone that has the tendency to make you smile on multiple levels; however, expectations must be set so both parties have an understanding. Without full disclosure of expectancies, chaos has the potential to creep in; therefore, avoid using alternative facts as a means to complete your quest.

Let's assume you meet the perfect individual and the chemistry is amazing! The face to face finessing begins! Take your time before jumping in with both feet because any form of dating comes with potential dangers and puts you at risk for victimization. Get to know the individual on a personable level. You don't want to find yourself developing feelings for a sociopath or psychopath because the end-result could become hazardous. When in the company of the person always observe his or her movements because the functionality of an individual tells a story about the person. Then you must be receptive to what it is you see and decide if it's something that you are willing to adapt to. Some people have mastered putting on a façade for the public, but the more time you invest in getting to know the individual will soon reveal who's hiding behind the mask.

Scenario: You're dating someone that has led you to believe that he/she has a consistent flow of income from business and legal hustles, but you later discover that the individual sells drugs sporadically to live day to day. There's no steady income, no house or car; however, the individual has ambitions of being a 'star' one day and you have seen the potential. Is that a situation that you are willing to place yourself in? Do you apply the 'no risk, no reward' mentality in this scenario?

Spending time and having fun is one thing, but imagine picking your friend up to hang out and he or she enters your vehicle with drugs. You have just been placed in a precarious situation. Is a little fun worth your freedom where you must unwillingly submit control of your life to authoritarians? I ask these questions because a simple quest for the booty can sometimes lead to a relationship. Should that be the case, then you must decide if it will be beneficial for you in the long run. In this scenario, I would suggest severing ties by any means because a person that cares about the well-being of others wouldn't place you in a situation that's none conducive to your lifestyle, especially without conferring with you first, not to mention, you're not even in a relationship with the individual. In my experience, if a person doesn't compliment who you are and has no sense of direction then he or she takes away from your value.

ONLINE VIRTUOSITY

It should come as no surprise that hookups and online dating are thriving in today's society. The like of a photo or stream of a video on social media can lead to some 'real time' fun. Also, there is an overabundance of dating websites made available to those seeking that approach. Online dating affords people the ability to converse with a multitude of people in a very short period of time which is an advantage that other avenues don't present. Although it comes with a variety of perks, there are also disadvantages with online dating. People can pretend to be whatever they desire online. I guess you have to take the bitter with the sweet with anything in life; however, it's important to be cautious when you delve into your online quest.

One of the more popular connections for casual dating is Instagram. The post of a cute picture (not referring to those that expose all your assets, leaving nothing to the imagination) but a normal picture can lead to numerous people from all walks of life sliding in your DM. In my experience, it has the tendency to get a little annoying, but hey, it's a sure-fire strategy if you are on the prowl. Of course, it would be foolish of me to forget about Facebook. It has been reuniting people for years and has opened doors for dating escapades.

Sure, you have a goal in mind when perusing the internet for the goodies, but there are likeminded individuals doing the same and the mask is on. You may be under the impression that you are communicating with a specific person only to find out later that it was nothing more than a façade. More importantly, you may find yourself being catfished! (duped, deceived, played)! I totally understand the need to satisfy the urge; however, in this day and time there are individuals out there that are piranha's. They will chew you up and spit out the pieces they don't like, so make your selection wisely.

    The mindset should not be that of a predator, instead, it should be that of a mature individual that can communicate effectively by stating his or her intentions. In doing so, you allow the other party to ponder the idea and make an informed decision about partaking in the quest. Never take an individual's choice away by being deceitful regarding your intentions because once the truth comes to light it can cause unwanted tensions in your life. Honesty is always the best policy in any given situation because it opens the door to endless possibilities. As stated earlier, the quest for the booty can lead to an unforeseen relationship. It is then you must decide, whether or not that individual will be beneficial to your quest. If your mindset is about winning and filled with positive vibes, you don't want anyone consuming your time and spreading negative energy.

CHAPTER 8

THE RELATIONSHIP

We've Explored Different encounters that sexual desires can lead to; however, sometimes we are blind-sided by our own ambitions for casual satisfaction that we become complacent, that is, until the unexpected occurs.

Casual sex or mingling occasionally leads to much more and causes us to feel baffled since it was never the intended purpose. Regardless to how hard we fight the feeling, emotions have a way of taking control.

In that instance, we find ourselves in a relationship. What type of relationship that may be is based upon what we open ourselves up to. It is then we must decide which direction it will go. An open relationship may be appealing to some whereas, others may be focusing on marriage.

Some relationships are simply meant to be, whereas others, well, not so much.

THE REBOUND

The rebound is the relationship that is more than likely destined to fail. Of course, this is debatable; however, when you find yourself leaving one relationship to enter another it generally means you bring that baggage along. Healing from those open wounds is necessary and time is needed to reflect on what could have been done differently from both parties. Reflecting allows you to clear your mind and focus on strengthening those weakened areas. In doing so, it will help you to avoid treading the same path resulting in another broken relationship. Immediately jumping into another relationship is a temporary fix that becomes more of a distraction as opposed to a relationship and it's not fair to the either party. Sure, moving on in a rebound relationship has the ability to help you forget what is left behind, but moving too fast when there are unresolved issues within will do nothing more than plague the new relationship you find yourself leaping into.

Naturally, when you think about the wasted time and energy you invested in the last relationship it sprouts a sense of urgency to find someone that will love and honor you; however, that is not always the case. Although you may want to move forward with someone new, the lingering pain is still present. Sure, it may be easy to mask the hurt, but that type of energy possess the ability to transfer over into the next relationship and what you think is hidden may be transparent to the other party.

If you desire to be in a relationship after a breakup then set the pace that is conducive to you healing from the last experience. Don't allow the next individual to take advantage of your vulnerability. Be mindful of the things you want from a relationship and do not place yourself in position to settle. Growth is an essential part of human nature and if you find yourself regressing, then you need to indulge in some alone time to further your growth. Figure out what it is you desire from a relationship and what you have to offer. Don't spend time searching for a partner, focus on the betterment of self and allow the potential partner to find you.

THE OPEN RELATIONSHIP

The open relationship affords couples the freedom to date and have sexual encounters with others. In other words, they are not exclusive. It may be a good fit for those who struggle with monogamy, yet still care for the significant other. Of Course, there are pros and cons as there are with anything in life. Why not have your cake and eat it too, right? Well, it can only work successfully when both parties reach an agreement about the levels of involvement with outside partners. Both must find a comfort level that's digestible when it comes to their partner engaging in sexual activity with a secondary partner that can possibly be better than what they receive at home. Imagine That!

    All open relationships are not just centered around outside sexual activity. Perhaps, there is a need for an emotional connection that hasn't been established or fulfilled in the current relationship, or maybe it just doesn't have the flare that it once had. Whatever the case, there should be specified perimeters about the rules of indulgence with other parties because spending too much time with a secondary partner is hardly propitious for the current relationship. Furthermore, the rules should be communicated prior to engaging in such activity. Based on experience, I've learned that honesty should always be a priority and each party should inform the other when they are seeing someone else. Of course, you should never date one another's friends, because that creates a mess all in itself and it defeats the purpose of having a successful open relationship. During this quest always use protection since monogamy is not a part of this equation. Wrap that thing up because it protects from unwanted diseases and pregnancies. With the rules in place there should be no jealousy; however, that is not always the case. After all, we are human and sometimes our emotions have the tendency to get the best of us.

Some of the pros of being in an open relationship are:
- You are not confined because you get to date other people
- You get to experience different sex styles
- You won't get bored easily
- You're available to explore other opportunities for a relationship
- No guilt because an understanding has been established

Some of the cons of an open relationship are:
- Managing time spent with different parties and having time for self
- Jealousy of partner being intimate with someone else
- Guilt may occur in spite of the established understanding
- Partner may part ways with you to be with someone else

Everything in life comes with a price; therefore,

look at both pros and cons and decide if an open relationship will place you in the necessary position needed for you to win.

FRIENDS WITH BENEFITS

A friend with benefits relationship can be a very liberating experience because you get to enjoy certain benefits without any strings attached. This type of relationship should not be done with a close friend that's near and dear, but perhaps with an acquaintance that you have established a certain rapport. The individual should not be someone you envision yourself being in a monogamous relationship with, rather someone you can have vigorous fun while enjoying the perks. Both parties need to have a full understanding of the terms to ensure they are on the same page to avoid the risk of anyone being hurt later.

    A friend with benefits is just that...a friend that provides some benefits. Keep the relationship restricted to just the benefits, but be sure to leave an impact that will allow you to always go back at the time of your choosing. Avoid daily communications because you don't want to give mixed signals and you won't find yourself offended if the other party does not make time for you. Trying to hang out or communicate daily causes blurred lines that neither party signed up for. Also, you want to avoid emotional attachments because this type of relationship is only to satisfy a need which should have been communicated upon initialization of the relationship. Sure, it's fine to have fun with the other party but do not allow him/her to hang around your family or friends on any occasion because he/she is meant to be temporary. If you allow your short-term escapades to intertwine with people that are closest to you then you are establishing a long-term connection. That is not the vision!

Enjoy the moments shared, but stay in control of the flow of things. Catching feelings is a no! Avoid it at all costs unless you both reach an agreement of exclusivity. Know your position and play it like it goes. Things should be very simple when it comes to a friend with benefits. In this type of relationship, you get to be selfish because it's all about you. Don't do dates in public settings because it's not your man or woman and you don't want to find yourself being linked to that individual in that capacity. Furthermore, do not and I repeat do not do sleepovers! Hang out, have fun, get what you came for and go home. There is no need for post sex cuddling. Save that intimacy and emotional bonding for the person you decide to be in a relationship with. Feel me?

Remember that having a friend with benefits gives the emotional freedom to explore your options until you meet the person with whom you are ready to be in a meaningful relationship. You are free to do you, so don't get mad or jealous if you see him/her out with someone else. It's not like you are being cheated on. The other party is simply exploring their options and so should you. Do whatever makes you happy and allow no one to predicate what that should be.

TOXIC RELATIONSHIP

A toxic relationship is by far the worst kind because more often than not, it may lead to abuse and perhaps even death. Many times, people in toxic relationships will not listen to the outcry of loved ones telling them to get out of it because they focus their attention on times that were good. By no stretch of the imagination can they conceptualize that it has become toxic. Various issues can factor into the deterioration of the relationship. Keep in mind that losing yourself by forgetting who you are and your aspirations because you've spent your time investing in your partner will eventually lead to resentment and negativity. Your total happiness should never be contingent on what your partner brings forth because dependency places you at the mercy of your partner; therefore, making you powerless. You should never forget to make your happiness a priority.

Codependency within the relationship can also be a form of toxicity because neither seem to function at normal capacity without the other. They find themselves doing things out of the ordinary to keep the other's love. That is not the foundation for which a relationship should be built because it hinders proper growth of each individual as well as the relationship. Partners should enhance one another's growth and it should always be on an upward trajectory; however, most toxic relationships do not work out that way. Years slip by and they have become stagnant because negative energy has consumed the relationship and they find themselves in the same position as when they started or worse.

Perhaps both partners have strong personalities, but one is a control freak. He/she dominates the relationship by setting all the rules and if the other disagrees it becomes a major issue causing the partner to feel as if he/she is walking on eggshells. Nothing that the partner does is good enough and it causes frequent disagreements. As the arguments progress criticism and contempt become more frequent causing the recipient to feel worthless. Once ignorance is uttered to devalue the partner sometimes an apology cannot repair it. The tone is set that there is no appreciation or respect so it puts the partner on the defensive and the cycle continues.

Have you ever been in the company of a toxic couple? Let me assure you that it's a terrible experience. It's like a never-ending battle. The couple that I'm referencing are both excessively jealous individuals and, purposely add to those insecurities by sleeping with other people to deliberately hurt one another. Those actions always lead to arguments that swiftly result in physical altercations. Police get involved yet they manage to stay together only to repeat the cycle. The fights are never ending and have sometimes resulted in trips to the ER. Abuse is never okay and as many times as they separate they find their way back to one another. No one cares to be around their shenanigans because they refuse to get the necessary help needed to aid in their rehabilitation. If you find yourself in a comparable situation, GET OUT! Leaving with your life, sanity and physicality is always better than leaving in a casket.

MISTRESS AKA SIDEPIECE

Women who have secret affairs with men that are in relationships or married are known as the mistress. In today's culture, the name has been duplicated and glorified as the side piece. Shockingly, women nowadays take pride being in that position and there is zero shame being the other woman. Here in Atlanta, we have a radio station that allows individuals to call in and give a shout out to their side piece. I was taken aback when I initially heard it and thought, damn, this is the world of today. I'm not here to pass judgement on anyone because at one point in time I played that position; that is, until I realized my worth. I came to the realization that in the game of relationships, I don't come off the bench, I start.

(Woman to Woman)

Some women may get involved with a guy believing she is the only woman because the guy may not have given full disclosure about his relationship status. If you don't know that's one thing; it's what you do afterwards when you discover the truth that matters. Do you continue to be his side piece or do you call it quits because he placed you in a compromising position? Regardless to any emotions that may have developed, your decision should be centered around morals, self-worth and integrity. The fact of the matter is you have the power to make a conscious decision and walk away. Should you decide to continue being the other woman just know that karma is not blind and eventually you will reap what you sow.

Let's not forget about the women that brag about being a side piece. Why, surely you jest! You can't possibly think you will be the exception to the rule. If he cheats on his girlfriend or wife with you, what makes you think you will not receive the same in return? Oh, because he said he loved you? I'm sure at one point he told his significant other the same thing and so the cycle continues. You're nothing more than his murky little secret. Furthermore, chances are you're only one of many options. Let's just use a hypothetic and say you are the only other woman. Does it give you comfort knowing that you're on borrowed time? To the bag chasing side piece it matters not because that type is in it for the monetary gain. Let's be real, your worth depreciates the moment you put a price on yourself. So, does that equate you to a prostitute? I'm just asking. Perhaps you're living on the hope factor. Hoping that he will leave his significant other for you so you can get more of the same. Hardly! In some instances that could very well be the case, but then you must ask yourself, what prize did you really get? Knowing the circumstances in how you got him will more than likely be the same way in which you lose him.

    Ladies, it's time to stop devaluing yourselves and take pride in who you are as women. If you can't make plans about your future together (other than in your head) then do not settle for being his in the meantime woman even if the perks are more than you can acquire with your own talents.

You should never allow someone to be your choice if you're nothing more than their option. There is someone for everyone, but you can't receive what's for you if you are busy losing yourself to a man that's committed to someone else. Always place yourself in position to win by not being blinded by tempestuous pleasures, especially those that will diminish your character. At the end of the day, those 'stolen' moments with him are going to cost you and the price may just be outside of your budget because karma does not discriminate.

MONOGAMOUS (DEDICATED) RELATIONSHIP

The monogamous relationship with two dedicated individuals seems like the pot of gold at the end of the rainbow in this day and time, but certainly achievable. It simply takes two people with the right mindset that love one another and refuse to allow anyone or anything to come between them. Easier said than done, right? Sure, there will be numerous challenges, but if you choose a partner that inspires you, respects you, allows you to be yourself, and has your best interest at heart then you're on the right path. Each party must be ready to establish a solid foundation that is built on trust, respect, understanding, honesty and loyalty. Another key element is learning your partner's personality. As trivial as it may seem, it's important to understand how to put a smile on his/her face when experiencing a trying moment or when to give him/her some alone time. More importantly, learning what motivates your partner builds a solid connection and keeps one another on track when you lose focus.

A successful monogamous relationship should not be built primarily on sex. That's a fact! There must be more substance than just great sex because eventually that goody good becomes the norm and creates a desire for exploration with outside sources. Of course, there is the lingering stigma that all men cheat, but that's not necessarily true because there are a few good men left somewhere in the world. A real man (no pun intended) can be satisfied with one woman that's not afraid of her sexuality and knows how to stimulate his body, heart, mind and soul. If for some reason he was not being satisfied sexually or emotionally and he was considering stepping outside of the relationship he would discuss alternatives with his woman prior to doing so in hopes of finding a solution. Furthermore, to avoid receiving any unwanted sexual or emotional help from an outside party within the relationship both partners must express their needs and desires with their partner so those needs are fulfilled. By all means, avoid betrayal at all costs because it destroys the trust and sometimes there is no resurrecting it.

    Open communication is a vital tool for having a healthy relationship because it allows you to address concerns with your partner which allows understanding to flow freely. There is something spectacular about being in a committed relationship because it allows you to grow with an individual. Then of course, you have the option to have unprotected sex and don't have to fret over contracting an STD. We all know there is nothing like peace of mind because it is then that you can thrive and reach your full potential. Establishing stability and security with someone you love while you both achieve your goals provides a sense of satisfaction that's indescribable. Being able to call or go home and share how your day went with your partner is well worth the sacrifice of being committed. If both parties are open to change and able to adapt to it for the betterment of the relationship then, it's destined to flourish. Also, they must be mindful that some things will not change; perhaps, it's those very things that placed the relationship in position to win in the first place. Finding true love in this day and era seems a bit illusive, but it's highly possible with the right companion.

LOST GIRL

Lost girl experienced her fair share of relationships. She was in search of the love that she never received from her father as a little girl and by golly, she was going to find it by hook or by crook. Not knowing her worth as a teenager she fell into the trap of being the side chic with her first love. As a young naïve teen, she realized she didn't like being the best kept secret and eventually didn't bother trying to hide it. She was in love and no one could tell her anything...not family, not friends, not even his main chic. Well, needless to say, that resulted in a fight with the girl. Eventually that relationship ended, but they remained the best of friends. He genuinely cared about her as a person and even showed up to her wedding when she ran off and got married at 18.

Before getting married, she stumbled along the way still trying to fill the void of love that she needed from her father, but to no avail. Instead, she settled for security with a guy 10 years her senior. She wasn't in love, but then again, she had no clue what love truly was. She was willing to give it a shot though because anything was better than returning to her mom's home to deal with the advances or physical abuse from her step-father. Unfortunately, she soon learned that betrayal was knocking on the door. Upon returning from her honeymoon, while visiting her sister-in-law, her husband received a call. He took the call and left shortly afterwards for what he claimed was a gas station run that lasted approximately 3 hours. About a week later his ex-woman wanted to ensure that Lost Girl knew that it was she that called that night and he came to meet her. She made it her business to communicate that they had sex.

    The guy that she learned to love had betrayed her. Of course, he denied it when confronted by both women, but the ex knew far too many details about that night starting with the phone call. She told the time he left his sister's, what he was wearing, how long he was gone, what he had on and when he returned. Just a coincidence? I think not! It was cemented in Lost Girl's mind that he betrayed her. She stayed with him for a few years despite his infidelity, but when opportunity presented itself she did not allow his infidelity to go unsettled. Unfortunately, men can't take it when the shoe is on the other foot. After numerous times of trying to make it work, they parted ways. Lost girl continued her mission to find love and actually found it from a country boy that was a few years younger. She lost all hope in older men since all she received from them was disappointment, starting with her father. Country Boy put no one before her and loved her tremendously. She could do no wrong in his eyes. She was smitten by him because of the way he loved her. Although she was in love with him, regrettably, she didn't know how to demonstrate it effectively.

Watching her mom be abused then being betrayed by her ex-husband spilled over into the relationship. She desperately wanted it to work with him because he showed her how a man was supposed to treat and love a woman. She had the want to, but unfortunately didn't have the know-how. After a few years of trying to make it work, it came to an end. That moment became one of regret that she continuously lives with to this day. She later realized that she should have fought harder to salvage the relationship. He's sometimes thought about especially when she hears R Kelly's song, Slow Dance (That was their song). It brings to her remembrance the love she took for granted when she was struggling to find her way. She went on with her life trying to figure out how to put the pieces together, but made continuous mistakes along the way. She eventually moved to the city where her father lived. Much to her surprise, that father-daughter relationship did not go as she had envisioned all those years as a little girl.

In spite of her endless pain, she still believed that someone was out there that could love her like Country Boy once did. She found herself mingling with the neighbor across the street. He was from New York and had a different swag. She was intrigued by him and eventually found herself in a relationship with him. Of course, daddy didn't approve, but at this point the damage by him was already done, yet she still attempted to establish a relationship with him. She became rebellious because she was quite desolate and somewhat broken. She had begun to internalize every emotion that she had experienced up to this point until she found an outlet that helped her to forget her pain for the moment. She turned to marijuana laced with cocaine. It became her escape away from the rejection of her father's love. It didn't do much for her relationship. Even though it was filled with love, it became a tumultuous battle.

Lost Girl directed her built-up frustrations and pain towards her New York love. He was taken aback because he did not understand where it was all coming from. The drugs intensified situations between the two and eventually it took a negative toll on the relationship which sometimes resulted in domestic issues. Things spiraled out of control and the issues superseded the love. Eventually Lost Girl decided to leave the drugs alone because more harm than good generated from it. She and Mr. New York tried to make it work for a few years, but they could never get their footing back because too much damage had been done. He returned to New York and she eventually ended up moving to the state where she was born and her mother now resided.

Her mom finally left her step-father so that gave her a sense of peace. After several broken relationships, she began to lose hope that she would find love again. She went about life trying to figure things out during her journey. Unfortunately, it was a struggle and she bumped her head along the way. It seemed even a short sweet romance would not last because her past transgressions would come back to haunt her. So, what was the point in believing that she could have happiness? She no longer valued relationships and didn't care about who got hurt in the process. In that moment, even a married man was fair game. Her judgement was cloudy and she became very selfish. Eventually, she came to the realization that she needed to make better decisions for her life. She learned to want more than just living in the moment because it always created turmoil.

One night while out partying at a little shot gun club (if that's what you would call it) she locked eyes with a guy that would impact her life forever. They decided they wanted to get to know one another better and started hanging out. He was younger and inexperienced with being a family-oriented person. She now had kids and he didn't; therefore, she was leery about letting her guard down. She had just bought her first home and wanted to live life comfortably without distractions. After all, she'd already had her fair share of broken relationships. He was wild and initially deceptive, but there was something about him that she couldn't shake. Likewise, he admired her tenacity and decided to get his act together.

He later moved in with her and they focused on making their relationship work. He was a hard worker and made sure things were taken care of at home. They were good together because they balanced each other and were determined on building a life together. After two years together, they were married and life was better than ever, that is, until some of his family members started to interfere and cause problems. During a brief separation, he stayed at a relative's house. It is then he stepped outside of the marriage and had an affair with his ex-girlfriend. Perhaps it happened prior to the separation because they hadn't had sex for a couple of months. They both worked different shifts and time did not permit. (we'll let that be the reason)

Lost Girl still didn't know about the affair until she and her husband decided to work things out and his ex-girlfriend called his cellphone. He was asleep and the calls continued, so Lost Girl finally answered and the ex-girlfriend wasted no time in telling Lost Girl that she had been intimate with her husband. She woke him up and asked what in the hell was she talking about. He shrugged it off and hung up the phone, but she continued to call. Lost Girl pleaded with him to tell her that he and his wife were back together. He eventually did, but in that moment the betrayal that she had known from the past came to the forefront. Having to plead with your husband to tell his ex-girlfriend, now mistress, not to call his phone changed the dynamics forever. Lost Girl did not respond to betrayal with open arms. She believed in sharing the pain. She was beyond hurt because this time she was in love and recognized it. When she took her vows before God, this time it was from her heart and for him to betray her in this manner, regardless to how much she loved him was unforgettable.

She had a friend who was incarcerated that had a ton of outside connections. She began to form a bond with him and even though they never had sexual relations he satisfied the emotional void that became prevalent during the downfall of her marriage. She remained with her husband, but taunted him every chance she got while talking on the phone with her friend. It ate at the core of her husband's being, but she didn't care because he cheated and then she had to plead with him to tell the female that he was back with his wife. What type of husband would put his wife through such emotional distress? He realized that he hurt her deeply and was fighting to make things right again, but the damage had been done. One day she took it to the fervent extent by having him drop her off at the jail to visit her friend while he and the kids went to the park until the visit was over. That was the dagger in the heart. They continuously tried to make it work. He even moved with her to another city because they lost their home due to a huge storm. She still taunted him and wouldn't let up.

   He decided that he would go back home to live with Lost Girl's family. One night she received a call from her brother proclaiming that he heard their sister on the phone with Lost Girl's husband discussing being together. That was the last straw. She called her family and demanded that they put him out INSTANTLY or there would be hell to pay! They were done. About a week or so later he ended up being an accessory to a crime that got him a couple of years in jail. Lost Girl stood by his side the ENTIRE time even when his family turned their backs. Why would she, when he hurt her to the core? The answer was simple, she still loved him and was seeing it through for better or worse. Upon his release, they tried to work it out for the sake of their marriage. They lived in two different states and it made things difficult. He later moved to where she was, but struggled finding work because of his record. Frustrations set in because of extra family members living in the household which caused a financial burden. He and Lost Girl got into an altercation which resulted in him going back home to be with his family. Periodically they tried to work it out, because the love was always there, but the distance, his public infidelities along with interference from his family would not permit it to be so. After a period of 9 years of going back and forth it was time to let go.

    Loving someone and understanding what it entails only to have that person break your heart is devastating. She only reaped what she had sowed in previous relationships in which there was no expiration date. Karma is not blind and repays in full what each person is owed. Lost Girl, had to go through those series of broken relationships to understand her value in this world. She needed to come to the realization that even though she was unable to cultivate a wholesome relationship with her father, she didn't need love from a man to validate her worth. It made her stronger, wiser and determined. It molded her into a self-sufficient queen with limitless options.

CHAPTER 9

THE FEAR & THE FAITH

THE FEAR

Fear Paralyzes Individuals from expanding their minds when facing new challenges. The sad thing is, fear does it so gracefully because many people don't comprehend why their ability to achieve has been hindered. It functions as a disabler and causes you to saturate your mind with negative thoughts. Fear will consume your being by using your weaknesses against you. Its sole mission is to stomp all over you causing you to lose focus. You should be conscious especially when it comes to fear because its conniving and will use your past as a means of control. You will hear the silent whispers in your mind reiterating that you're not good enough.

Fear wants you to feel hopeless and helpless. What you need to understand is when you submit to fear, you lose! Fear becomes the victor and your hope and aspirations become smothered because the mind is consumed with despair and eventually hope and aspirations become but a distant memory. Fear is so bold that it will create problems where there need not be any. Its job is to manipulate you into thinking that your past failures are indicative of your future success. LIES! Just because you fall, it doesn't mean you should remain there. Get up, dust yourself off, collect your thoughts and start over.

Do not allow fear to be an impediment to your progress! Sometimes our misconceptions of situations will act as a deterrent all because we allowed fear to build a home in our minds. It can sometimes create debilitating anxiety that may require professional treatment.

Shield your mind and thoughts from fear, otherwise, it will impose limitations upon your ability.

Example: You desire to try a new business endeavor, but you're afraid because your last attempt was an epic fail. It simply did not go as planned because you were not prepared. You struggled alone to keep it afloat but did not have sufficient funding. This time you've done the required research, wrote your business plan, and even found a location that's great for your target audience. You've shared your ambitions with a friend and he/she wants to be an investing partner, because the potential to generate revenue is easily visualized. Do you allow fear from your past failure to dictate what could be one of the greatest moments of your life? Of course not! You've already done most of the leg work and this time you have support from someone else. Step out on faith because nothing beats a failure but a try.

    You will need to dig deeply within to muster up some courage to confront fear directly. Start by filling your mind with positive thoughts because fear is the wall that stands between you and your dreams, but faith is the antidote to destroying it. Furthermore, faith has the capability to devoid fear of it its power and place you on the correct path to becoming a better you. Overcoming fear through faith is vital to your success.

THE FAITH

Faith is one of the most essential components needed to thrive. Regardless to what stage we're at in life, faith allows us to believe in the impossible. Instead of allowing negative energy to control our thought patterns, faith delivers hope, that if we only believe, anything is possible. Some of you may ask, who or what is it that we need to have faith in. What or who you decide to have faith in is solely up to you, whether it's having faith in God, in yourself, your capabilities, or someone else, you need to have faith in something because it's a lifeline to help you through the most wearisome times in life. Faith alleviates doubt and gives you strength to be all that you can be because it establishes complete confidence.

Faith was designed to neutralize fear, but we must be careful not to react to fear, but instead, respond to it. Reacting to fear is instinctual and that's when it positions itself to become a threat. When we respond with faith we make a conscious choice to deal with it accordingly. It provides a form of stability within our minds which transforms our thought patterns. Furthermore, faith will allow us to do things we never deemed ourselves capable of doing because it affects how we view reality. Consequently, fear will cause us to view people and situations as threats to our significance, whereas, faith allows us to form a perspective to confidently look at them as opportunities. Now that's something to think about!

When it comes to dealing with people in our everyday lives, sometimes it's hard to let our guards down and expose our vulnerabilities, but it is then we must put our faith to use. On occasion, we will be faced with adversity because people are not perfect and prone to mess up which could result in us being hurt. When that occurs, we must rely on faith to help us overcome. Sure, it's easier said than done, and I'm the first to admit it. I would rather just cut them off and keep it moving and in some instances, that is the case; however, it's not applicable in all situations. That's why we must learn to walk by faith and not by what we see because human nature can sometimes cloud our judgement.

Learning to live by faith is sometimes challenging, but it's necessary. We must exercise our faith daily in everything we do. When we are driving a vehicle, we must have faith that we are going to make it to our destination safely without incident. When we catch a flight, we must have faith that it's not going to crash. The same applies when we are trying to accomplish our goals. We must have faith that each will come to fruition. Make no mistake, we must still put in the necessary work to see those goals become reality because faith without works is dead. (James 2:20)

My Views: Sometimes it seems like gravity pulls some of us down and it's hard to rise above it, especially with the senseless things that are taking place in the world. People hate others they've never even met because of the color of their skin (racism at its finest). Police officers are being viewed as public enemy number one by many because some of them choose to spill innocent blood without accountability. Someone that took a knee for something in which he believed is now being ostracized by an organization. Agendas are being pushed to dismantle and ultimately destroy a group of people. If you refuse to be silent, they label you as non-compliant, hostile and defiant. I don't understand nor do I accept the rationale for such ideocracies because I'm conscious of the degradation that's being placed upon a specified race; therefore, I reject their deposit.

When you turn a blind eye to those being oppressed, it makes you no better than the oppressor. Love knows no color. Stand in unison, make a thunderous roar, and have faith that tireless efforts will evoke change. Our youth are being exterminated simply by walking to the store or going to school and no one is held accountable. Refuse to be silenced! You cannot win if you do not fight! Stop accepting the frivolous ideologies as logic just because they say it's justifiable. Have faith that changing a flawed system starts with **YOU**. Never ask permission to be treated as equal; only ask forgiveness for the collateral damage that gets in the way. The power is in the people;

therefore, be silenced no more! Despite the madness and the many distractions, have faith that God will allow us to knock down the door because fear is not of Him.

CHAPTER 10

THE GROWTH (THE W)

GROWTH AND DEVELOPMENT

Becoming A Better individual is all about growth and development. Conducting a full assessment of your strengths and weaknesses will help you to discover the importance of improving those characteristics that do not bring value to your being. You should also learn from past mistakes made and work towards implementing change. Life lessons will allow you to go through the transformation process, because what doesn't kill you will definitely make you stronger. It's necessary to first understand that we all have flaws in our character and perfection is not attainable; however, figuring out what you want out of life places you on the correct path. Perhaps, something or someone has inspired you to improve and empower yourself; it is now up to you to figure out what path you must take. Whatever the case, it is your duty to reach your full potential, because wondering throughout life aimlessly hinders you from finding meaning and purpose in yourself.

Don't make the mistake of trying to structure your life based on someone else because you are unique; therefore, your growth will differ from the next. Your purpose will begin to form when you set realistic goals then set out to achieve them. Your life's purpose should not only be beneficial to yourself, but to others as well. When you are able to help others live a more virtuous life, then you have created a pathway for them to embark on their journey. Will it be an easy feat? I seriously doubt it. By no means be discouraged because growth can be derived through adversity. Adversarial growth does require some faith and resilience. You must believe that you can achieve anything you set your mind to doing. In doing so, you can adapt to change and overcome challenges effortlessly.

THE 'W'

The path to getting the W can be challenging in many ways, but the result is a more meaningful and satisfying life; which will be manifested in your self-image, confidence, place of work or business, relationships, lifestyle, as well as your views. Once you reflect on your life, you must examine the areas of growth and figure out what impact you want to make in the world. If you struggle with low self-esteem, then direct your attention to absolving yourself of that limitation. Once you can acknowledge your worth, you will be able to function at a higher level. Whatever limitations in your life that are hindering your growth and causing you to be ineffective, free yourself from it.

    Once you liberate yourself from the brazen restrictions that limit your productivity, it's important to gain a full understanding of your desires because it will create a sense of direction and allow you to develop a vision. After you establish the essential elements of your vision, you must put in the necessary work to turn it into reality. It is such an amazing feeling to see your vision come to life! We all have the potential to be anything we desire if we refrain from placing restraints on ourselves. A true visionary sets direction for change without deviating from the set purpose. It's all about placing yourself in the right position and dropping anchor at the precise moment because unfortunately, some conflicts are inevitable. As long as you are able to constructively handle those struggles, then you are on your way to do amazing things.

I almost forgot about Lost Girl. Let's talk about her, shall we? She spent numerous years trying to find her way, but once she understood her worth, she was able to walk into her purpose. She flourished and became a very intelligent and passionate woman, especially when it concerned affairs of the heart. Her loyalty knows no end unless you betray her (old habits die hard I guess). Do not misconstrue her kindness for a weakness, because she still has the ability to be fierce and unapologetic.

As an adolescent she loved to write, but somehow life always got in the way. Nowadays, she's a published author that's full of charisma and dedicated to being an inspiration to those that are open to suggestion. Against all odds, she became someone she was proud to face in the mirror. She learned the hard way that acquiring the W was the culmination of hard work, dedication and tenacity. I watched Lost Girl grow to become an amazing woman. No one knows her better than I, because she and I are one in the same.

END NOTES

Chapter 2
Petty Betty is found on urban dictionary.com as a reference to an individual that is too extra or perpetually petty.

Chapter 3
1. Loaded Lux vs Calico at Summer Madness 2, During Lux verse, he asked Calico was his money being long worth his life span being shorter. Can be found on YouTube.

2. Tupac Shakur, Me against the World lyrics: 1995. I know it seems hard sometimes but remember one thing, through every dark night, there's a bright day after that. So, no matter how hard it get, stick your chest out, keep ya head up and handle it.

ABOUT THE AUTHOR

Indy Lindsey relocated to Atlanta, Georgia after life as she knew it, was uprooted by Hurricane Katrina. She was determined to make a better life for her family no matter how long it took. As a youth, she loved to write and had inspirations of becoming a writer; however, a tumultuous life overshadowed those dreams. Coincidentally, one day while joking with her sons, her passion for writing, which had become a faded memory, manifested itself through vision. She began her quest by creating material that was indicative of overcoming adversity through personal experience or affiliation. She shares pieces of her story within the book in hopes of constructing relatable and demonstrative bridges of the overview. Passion, which is displayed throughout is one of her stronger attributes. This is not the last you will hear about Indy Lindsey. She's just getting started!

113 • Quest For The W